GW01218069

Pandora's Bc

a collection of light verse by Lynn Roberts
drawings for cover and illustrations by Lynn

Rob and
Sue
X X X X X X X

Twelve poems from this collection have been published in the web magazine
Lighten Up Online at various times – with thanks to Martin Parker

www.lynnroberts.co.uk

published by InVerse
16 Grove Hill Gardens, Tunbridge Wells TN1 1SR

ISBN: 978-0-9567806-1-4

Pandora's Book

a collection of light verse

and drawings by

Lynn Roberts

CONTENTS

PART I –THE CLASSICAL SECTION

PART II – THE LITERARY SECTION

Two early poems by famous poets:

Two publishers' rejections of the works of famous poets:

Two thankyou letters from poets for unsuitable gifts from their fans:

EPILOGUE: An allegorical tragedy in 100% polyester

.

Part I -

THE CLASSICAL SECTION

Ο
δεαρ...

ΟΜΕΡΟΣ

Pandora's Book

Aphrodite explains the unfortunate affair with Ares

It was just *flirt*ing. It was very slight.
We met one evening in a clouded bar;
he was the sort of man I liked on sight –
we'd have some fun; we wouldn't go too far.

We met one evening in a clouded bar;
he bought me wine and I bought him champagne.
We'd have some fun; we wouldn't go too far
as I was married – I made that quite plain.

He bought me wine and I bought him champagne.
He was a soldier, home on leave, he said,
and I was married, I made that *quite* plain –
I wouldn't let my heart control my head.

He was a soldier – home on leave, he said
(he was extremely tall and fit and strong);
I wouldn't let my heart control my head,
although my heart glissandoed in a song.

He was extremely tall and fit and strong
(my husband's strong – although he's rather lame);
he made my heart glissando in a song;
I only meant to have a little game.

My husband's strong – although he's rather lame;
he works a forge, a man of soot and iron.
I only meant to have a little game;
I never meant to stir a sleeping lion.

He works a forge, a man of soot and iron,
but still he seemed to see my secret heart;
I never meant to stir a sleeping lion –
I thought I'd kept my different lives apart.

He seemed to see into my secret heart.
He found us one day – it had gone some way;
I thought I'd kept my different lives apart;
they touched, and it no longer seemed like play.

He found us one day – it had gone some way.
He caught us in a pixel-woven maze;
we touched – but it no longer seemed like play:
he filmed us – for his friends to see, he says.

He caught us in a pixel-woven maze –
it was just *flirt*ing; it was very slight.
He *filmed* us – for his friends to see, he says!
... and he had been a man I'd *liked*, on sight.

Blogged down

Oh, it's morning on Olympus and each Muse has donned her frock;
they are waiting for Apollo – they are looking at the clock –
but Apollo's in the bathroom with a chronic writer's block.

His novel's hit the bollards down on Inspiration Road;
there's an arid little desert where his fluency once flowed;
his verse is in reverse and there's an O which should be ode.

Apollo thought his Muses could hardly be much breezier;
'O gods,' he cried, 'What's wrong with me? Perhaps I've got amnesia?'
Euterpe said, 'Well, try a blog – I'm sure you'll find it easier.'

Apollo got connected – now he's blogging night and day;
his lyre stands idle on the shelf while he describes the way
a string has snapped, and how he's got a satyr he must flay.

He catalogues each mortal ache in his immortal knee;
discusses all the deer he's killed and adds a recipe,
and speculates which god's amour has changed into a tree.

The nymph of the Pierian spring has packed up in disgust;
the epic bards are trudging north – it's Hrothgar's court or bust!
Apollo's deathless arrows (like his prose) are cloaked in dust.

Oh, save us from another blog, which seven people read;
how many of us need to know your goldfish doesn't feed? –
or how your lawn (and perhaps your brain) has really gone to seed?

The zero in the comments box reveals the utter ted-
ium of this infernal craze – this horrid virtual screed;
pull out the plug, O Muse, before our eyeballs start to bleed...
close down, Control/ Alt and Delete – Apollo must be freed!

Epicurius and the solution to economic downturn

I hymn the ham... I have a hunch the answer to a lot is lunch
(which saves the world and shores it up);
sometimes the only way is sup.

Oh, when the banks (in days of old) were foursquare, strong, replete
with gold,
the bankers sat from noon till three
amid a tide of napery,

discussed the dollar, dealt the deal and never made a mongrel's meal
of sub-primes or the loans they lent -
benignly in control, content.

But now they work from six till nine on tofu rolls, eschewing wine,
the house of cards has tumbled down:
it's bread and tears for Mr Brown*.

My friend and I have lunch (sans men); what keeps us going is the ben-
ison of tapas and prosecco –
laudamus! cheers! the walls re-echo!

A hex on cold Sobriety (her self-denial, her greenish tea) –
lunch long and raise your glass on high:
the symbol of success is   !

*This rhyme is subject to political variation.

Maenadness

Where should I be without you? –
you are strong and dark and wild;
when I'm with you I am happy
and as careless as a child.

You are teasing; you can sparkle;
you are young and you are green;
when you touch my lips I blossom;
you are earthy – you are clean.

Quite often you are fruity
and frequently you're dry;
you can make me sing or silent,
make me giggle, make me cry.

I hunger for your body;
you smell of peach and musk;
I look for you at noon, and
I pine for you at dusk.

You are chilled and you are golden,
you are rich and you are deep;
you woo me into ecstasy
and soothe me into sleep.

You get me through catastrophes
with children, work and cash;
you're amusing, you're my muse; you
inspire me in a flash.

Though I'm fickle, though I'm faithless,
vino veritas – it's true;
you're the god that I came in with,
Dionysos – I'm with you.

Bacchus and Ariadne, with the help of Titian

Actaeon and Diana

He stalks on padded feet, questing his prey,
hefting his camera, poised to shoot, his tread
delicate over leaves, gentling his way
into the garden's heart... the prize in reach. - Instead,
he trips – a dog barks - looking up, he stares
straight at the star he thought to catch; her eyes
ignite, her pale flesh smoulders and she flares,
a naked exocet; goddess of death. He shies:
she grips his camera, hurls it in the pool;
bodyguards pounce and drag him to the gate;
he sprawls across the tarmac, sorry fool,
where recently he strutted, blessed by fate.
His colleagues catch the scent of blood; as one
their lenses turn on him; his day is done.

Pallas Athene laments the judgment of Paris

Hera, girl, here's what I think – we should go and have a drink.
Once again, by Fate's fell plan, we've been sodomized by man.

How did we accept this con? – standing here with nothing on,
whilst a shepherd boy debates which of us he really rates.

Queen of heaven, Wisdom's ark – but completely in the dark,
even thinking we've a chance against Aphrodite's glance.

I have never felt so daft – up a creek without a raft –
while Paris, with his arms akimbo, leers at that immortal bimbo.

How could he have passed *you* over? - bride of Zeus and supernova –
seeing rosy Dawn define every (very queenly) line?

As for me, I'd dumped my glasses, bathed myself in milk of asses
(though I know my curves are meagre, men have always seemed
quite eager).

But – with fanfare and kerfuffle (calculated most to ruffle
every feeling of her peers) – Aphrodite then appears,

trailing doves and paparazzi, Paris as her willing patsy;
wearing nothing but a smile, unadorned but cloaked in guile.

Though her lips would not melt butter, I have heard a sneaky mutter
intimating that she wrought him round her little finger; bought him

with the bride of Menelaus, thus precipitating chaos:
years of war by rival forces, Grecian fire and Trojan horses.

Once again, by Fate's fell plan, lust has left us in the can.
Hera, girl, here's what I think: we should go and have a drink...
     or perhaps two...
        or even three...

The judgment of Paris, with input from Rubens and Botticelli

The goddess Hera commiserates with Mrs Tiger Woods

What do you do when your husband's a god
and he can't keep his glory wrapped up?
Do you sit down and cry? do you turn a blind eye
to the demiurge urges to tup?

What do you do when your husband's a god
and he keeps sneaking out on the prowl? -
prowling hither and yon disguised as a swan
and as various species of fowl?

What do you do when your husband's a god
with all the cute girls in his hand?
When, changed to a bull, he is pulling the wool
over every man's eye in the land?

What do you do when your husband's a god
who cavorts in Niagaras of gold?
It's no manner of use with immortals like Zeus
to attempt to reclaim them, I'm told.

So here's what I do (as my husband's a god,
and he can't keep his glory in check):
I've got an agenda of suitable men to
invite on a bender; the young and the slender
who'd like to befriend a deity; tender,
not scared of her splendour; who'd like to attend her –
perhaps to defend her (respecting her gender)...

...but basically wanting to neck.

An answer to CS Lewis's poem against cosmetics
('...& God did more than lipstick can to justify your mouth to man')

With morning face I wait the train
(a glistening nose and piggy eyes),
to find a seat to work the rites
which cause my Venus to arise.

I worship her with colour, cream
- with everything I should despise ;
with powder, mirror, brush and scent,
I conjure Freya to arise.

I do not care that I've been freed
from pleasing men; I realize
to ape my ideal self will please
my inner Aphrodite's eyes.

Though men may think that they prefer
an untouched skin and natural eyes,
the girls they pick are those who, like
Aglaia, see truth sometimes lies.

My friend, who boasts she stays the way
she wakes, affecting to despise
all Brangwyn's works, has weathered more
than some, less pretty but more wise.

And so I settle in the train,
set out my tools and close my eyes,
make a libation in my mind
and conjure Hathor to arise.

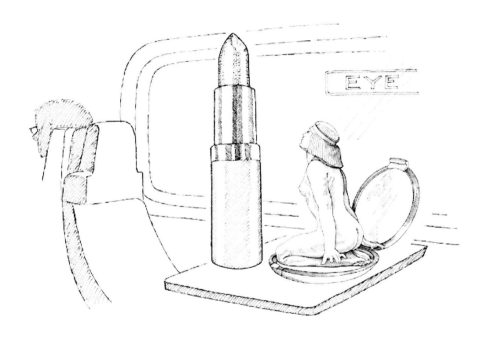

The worshipper, with some intervention by Allan Wyon

NB I do normally wear a little more than this when commuting

A Daughter is the Time of Truth
(with apologies to Aulus Gellius*)

You think that, when your daughter's born, you're getting Beth or Jo,
Matilda – Florence Nightingale – Grace Darling – I don't know.
You think that you're providing a happy childhood heaven
for Rapunzel, Cinderella – and you may be, till eleven...
then the hormones are recruited and start marching and deploying,
seize and occupy your sofa, which they fortify, destroying
your rest and peace and comfort; and you realize Medea
has invaded, with her colonels Clytemnestra, Boadicea.
Sarah Berhardt's in the kitchen and there's drama in the sink;
Messalina's on the doorstep, overcome by love (and drink),
and Jezabel is welded to the bathroom looking-glass
whilst Imelda's in hysterics 'cos her wardrobe's just too sparse.
You think that when your daughter's born you've got a little pet; –
you've got a whole menagerie, and it's not over yet:
you may be knocking on a hundred and hunkered in a hole,
but you know a daughter is for life - and you don't get parole.

(* who insisted perversely that Truth is the Daughter of Time)

Part II –

THE LITERARY SECTION

Two early poems by famous poets

1.

Death in Leamington
by John Betjeman aged 12 ½

I died upstairs in my bedroom
by the headlights of lorry and car
that shone through the open curtains
driving to Leamington Spa.

On the floor my pile of homework
was mountainous, deep and wide,
but although I should have done it
I was much too occupied.

And Mum crept by on the landing
as carefully as a mouse;
she did not know the Russians
were rushing about in her house.

I stared at the turbulent screen –
my crimson exploding head –
then I switched off *Call of Duty*
and scrambled into my bed.

2.
Sea fever
by John Masefield Year 5

I'm going down to the sea today to the big flat beach and the sand
and all I want is a big spade and a bucket in my hand
a ball to kick and a funny song in the car as we're arriving
and no police along the road in case my mum is driving.

I'm going down to the sea today to get sand underneath my toes
and bury Dad in a big hole right up until his nose
and all I want is a sunny day with big waves crashing
and to drown my little sister when she won't stop splashing.

I'm going down to the sea today to my mum's best picnic lunch
to a ham roll and a cheese roll with some sand for an extra crunch
and all I want is a big ice cream and a murdered pirate's skull
a small crab a jar of shrimps and a dead seagull.

Two publishers' rejections of the works of famous poets

1.

Jnᵒ. Milton, Esq.: - Sir,

I profess that I am honoured by the Advent of your Opus
(dramatically titled, and most promising in Topos);
the Porters who delivered it were virile, strong and able;
they have left it where it makes a most delightful Coffee Table.
I have cast an Eye upon it and have formed a firm Opinion
which I wish to give in Person (not to leave it to some Minion).
The Op'ning's very rousing, but it drops off when in Eden,
since nothing ever happens – neither Violence nor Breedin'.
Your Subject's irreproachable in Language, Source and Theme, and
I might be, Sir, more Sanguine if your Hero weren't a Demon.
You have given *him* the Action and the most poetic Verse
(see 'the Leaves in Vallombrosa', and much more I could rehearse).
If you make the Good so boring and the Wicked so alluring
your Work will not be published, let alone be prov'd enduring,
and your Ears will fast be forfeit to the Anger of the Church;
forgive yr Humble Servant – I must leave you in the Lurch.

2.

A Telephone Call from Mr John Murray

"You are dull, Mr Wordworth," the publisher said,
and your verse is the obverse of light; -
and yet you incessantly send me your poems;
do you think, on the whole, this is right?

"In your youth, why, perhaps you had some excuse
for a rhyme-scheme so plain and banal,
but now you are grown there's no place for this drone. -
Look at Byron!" he said, with a snarl.

"You are through, Mr Wordsworth," the publisher said,
"The age of Romantics is here;
the girls want a corsair, not shepherds in horsehair;
you're drab and provincial, I fear.

"In your youth you were wild and revolting in France,
but the clouds of your glory are over,
and I've had enough of leeches and stuff –
Lord Byron has put me in clover."

Two thankyou letters from poets for unsuitable gifts from their fans

1.

The Moan of the Ancient Rimester

Dear 'Fan' [it was a damsel fair
who sent to STC],
by all I own, this 'mobile phone' –
now wherefore giv'st thou me?

'Motion' and 'sound', its mongrel name? –
and yet it has no motion;
it's idle as an empty mind
with neither nous nor notion.

But oh! its sound – its sound is shrill;
the shrieking of a scold,
with lights which blink at me, and wink;
it thicks my blood with cold.

I try to write, but then, the fright! –
this screaming, eldritch warlock!
Please take it back, before I crack,
O fiendish Fan from Porlock!

2.
Ode to a microwave, by John Keats

My head aches and a dreadful numbness pains
my sense, as though of absinthe I had drunk,
injected meths or Dettol in my brains
one minute past, and on the floor had sunk.
'Tis not in despite at thy happy gift,
nor being too happy in a gift so bright,
that I, in this malodorous drift
of sulphurous yolk and white which smells like skunk,
weepeth and waileth in full-throated fright.
O for instructions! for this strange machine,
this tiny cooker, with its perilous power
to cook a banquet in a blink of e'en,
and leave me free to hymn the musk-rose flower;
how should I know that it wast never made
to warm the avian orb like easeful Death?
O, might I fly, and leave the smell to fade;
dear sir, I'm left forlorn, with no more breath....

John Keats,
slightly after Joseph Severn

THE PROBLEM PAGE:
Today, Internatural Marriage

Dear Dr Problem,
          Please help me! I confess I am quite at a stand...
I married a bountiful banker, but – fatally – Fate took a hand.
Three weeks out of four are idyllic, but (like credit) they vanish too soon;
that time of the month comes around, and my spouse starts to bay at the moon.

His hair blocks the pipes in the bathroom, his claws scrabble holes in the sheet,
and his *breath*! – well, you wouldn't believe it! – as his diet is mostly raw meat.
He won't stay to heel when we're walking; he chases small girls if they're fat;
he has eaten three pugs and a corgi, and I think that he's had next door's cat.

I've had to invest in a poop-scoop of four times the regular size,
and I've tried several times to de-flea him, but the powder gets into his eyes.
I'd quite like a dear little doggie, but *this* one...! – well, what can I say?
Would it help if I got him – well – *seen* to? or perhaps I should end it today?

But he *is* such a good little earner; he's bought me a farmhouse in Kent which turns my friends *green* when they see it... Oh! I thought that our marriage was *meant*.
Then the question of cubs – I mean, *babies* – well, what can I do about that?
Please help me...

       Yours very sincerely,

       Anna Whair-Wulff (née A. Ffampigher-Bhatt)

Taking doggy for a stroll, with thanks to *Vogue*

Song for a dark man

Where do you go to, my darling,
when the dawn creeps over the hill?
when the bullocks are stirring, the railways yawn
and the creatures of night are still?
Do you hang your cloak in the wardrobe?
Do you put your teeth in a glass?
Do you stretch out on silken padding
and wait for the daytime to pass?

Where do you go to, my darling,
when the stars fade into the sky?
when the bats are hung on the bat rack
and the milkman's float putters by?
Do you shut your eyes on the morning?
Do you pull down a lid on the day?
And does blood trickle over your smile
as the world wakes up to its play?

Where do you go to, my darling,
when the night has stabled his mare?
- when the pubs vomit out the carousers,
and Farming Today hits the air?
Do you slip on your black silk pyjamas?
Do you get M.R. James from the shelf,
and pour out a nice Nuits St Georges?
Do you like having time to yourself?

Where do you go to, my darling,
when the moon sails into the blue;
when the owls have finished their owling -
and why can't I go there too?
Do you have a quick drink on the way there?
Are you taking your work home as well?
Is your briefcase concealing a virgin?
Then you can go (darling) to hell.

Celebrity Santa chats exclusively to *Hello!* magazine!

Santa is having a lifestyle revamp
(Gok Wan is his new bestest chum);
he has chucked out the velvet and ermine,
and laid out a ginormous sum

on bright scarlet jeans from Armani,
with red Prada shoes like the Pope,
and a Gaultier hoodie (vermilion;
his colours are lacking in scope).

He has bought a resplendent Ferrari,
and pensioned off Rudolph et al;
his sack's now a Birkin (it goes with his jerkin)
– a freakishly costly fal-lal.

Santa's been reading GQ magazine;
he's shaved his moustache and his beard;
his hair's looking carefully windblown,
and he's looking just slightly weird

(what with collagen implants, veneers on his teeth,
and eyelash and eyebrow tattoos,
and Botox and waxing and facial relaxing,
and lipgloss the shade of his shoes).

Santa has mortgaged his igloo
to keep up with the fashion elite,
and he's now pretty skint as he's laid out a mint
on champagne & cocaine to compete;

so the prospect of stockings next Christmas
is just now decidedly bleak,
'cos – as well as the elf-abuse charges
-   well, Santa's in rehab next week.

Shakespeare's Missing Sonnet, Revealing the Identity of the Dark Lady

Shall I compare thee to my other half? –
thou art more curvy, and more passionate,
and hath a way always to make me laugh;
your summer, unlike hers, of youthful date.
Sometime so clear Apollo's whisper sounds,
but ofttimes is his inspiration blurred;
my dear co-author, how your brain abounds
with plot and character, with line and word.
Our sweetest times with parchment spent and quill;
your hair, as dark as ink, scrawls on my heart,
provoking strange excitement of the will,
and creativity in every part.
Oh, leave me not to Time's fell hand forsaken,
but stay to egg me on, sweet Frances Bacon.

The Lament of the Unplaced Poet

I'm stuck in the bowels of the shortlist,
shut out by Elysium's door;
I'm lurking in poetry's hallway
with the refusés pacing the floor.
We've made it as far as the doormat
and the vestibule's marble embrace,
but to enter the sancta sanctorum
requires a new level of grace.
They have pinned up the list on the lintel;
they are having a party inside;
the judge has selected his lambkins,
and I'm once more the maid, not the bride.
I tell all my friends it's subjective –
the judge's own personal taste –
then I fume and stick pins in his model,
till – lo and behold! I am placed! –
and the judge is expressing the zeitgeist
(expressing it terribly well),
and I walk through that door and I close it
on the doom-panelled hallway from hell...
(till the next competiton).

EPILOGUE

An allegorical tragedy in 100% polyester

A bra that's washed is never white as in its days of newness,
and oh! those days – those snowy days – are noted for their fewness.
If you can buy a dress of lights or one which shrugs the dirt off,
why not a bra which doesn't make you fear to take your shirt off?

A well-washed bra, you can't deny, is greyer than the weather...
its virgin white has leached away as snow melts from the heather;
yet T-shirts which start out as grey, with every wash get lighter
(I wish that *I* could, when I shower, increasingly grow brighter).

My fate, however, lours on me – a bit of a dismayer -
though colour-rinsing manfully, I, like my bra, grow greyer.